THE HERRING LASS

MICHELLE CAHILL
The Herring Lass

2016

Published by Arc Publications
Nanholme Mill, Shaw Wood Road,
Todmorden OL14 6DA, UK
www.arcpublications.co.uk

978 1910345 76 4 (pbk)
978 1910345 77 1 (hbk)
978 1910345 78 8 (ebk)

Cover illustration: 'The Fisher Girl, 1894' (oil on canvas),
Homer, Winslow / Mead Art Museum, Amherst College, MA, USA
Photo © Bridgeman Images

This project has been assisted by the Australian Government
through the Australia Council, its arts funding and advisory body.

Arc International Poets
Series Editor: James Byrne

In memory of
Lyn Hatherly (1945-2016)

CONTENTS

I hold you fast, until you are flesh again,
seal-herder, seer, sea-guardian:
you who can only tell the truth,
show me how to find a fresh wind
and a safe harbour.

ROBIN ROBERTSON

THE HERRING LASS

Not far from the stone harbour, herring kilns
pump wood smoke, smudged into an enterprise of masts
and the hemp rigging of a whole fleet, outward bound.

Her knife flashes in four-second strokes,
her wet hands never stray from a salted barrel.

There are knots in her scarf, the size of a child's fist.
She counts each silver piece, tossed over the shoulder.
Eye, hand and index finger outwit the boundless sea.

All day, men bustle in the courtyard, children stray.
A blacksmith smites metal, fishermen wait on a shilling,
whittle a stick along the wall, no word exchanged.

She tramps from port to port, from Crail to Pittenween.
The day unfinishing, her children yet to be fed,
the sailmaker, cooper, boat builder have all prospered.

She stands by a trough in the dark, guttering cold.
Black hulls heel under press of lugsails, foremasts low.
They drift with shoals of migrant herring the sea returns.

Because there are no shoals of haddock spawning,
he spends the night cutting timber to repair a keel,
gathers faggots in spit rain, in floodwater fields.

The sun's parachute silk settles over chimneys.
Pale clouds hang crowding the sky like driftnets.
Up, up, the black-backed gulls arc into draughts.

A heron hunched on the rocks like an old fisherman
in a raincoat snubs the hushed foray. The tide measures
time as autumn cobbles a town, deserted by tourists.

Dawn tarnishes roofs, their curved gables, furred
winter trees. Safe from saltmarsh, the intervallic
hedgerowed fields, he unloads bags of firewood.

He is not the sea's signature, its memory of human
coal, its middle passage of linen, tobacco, gold.
When beckoned, he leaves the harbour quietly.

The traveller enters the banal to haunt the empty
creels, his seaweed hair. She hears in a pipe rinsing
flagstones, Zambia's swamps – all the drowned past.

All winter they slept at Skara Brae,
their brochs empty. They dreamt of ivory,
an afterlife. They fed their herds grain.

When they woke, Romans had marched to
the stone forts of the mainland; *gromatici*
brought staffs, grids and a Senator's remittance.

But there was no caesura, no straight lines
at the edge of Empire. The wall was porous,
grafted, a marlstone coursing between firths.

It was like Palestine or Berlin, in theory,
a decumanus dividing tribes, farmlands, lords.
Libations for new gods, bright silver coins,

the frontier subsidies. Surveyors reckoned
the lie of land in turf, in clay numerics.
But nothing could drive out the Barbarians.

INSIDERS, AFGHANISTAN

(Australian War Memorial)

A swathe of poppies, a memorial to Darafshan,
        a father's odium for the rogue soldier.
In dust-winged chaos, machine-guns strafed at
        zero-hour, NATO games unplugged.
Those privates targeted by the Q&A talkback
        (Was the insider Taliban or insurgent?)
Did the sapper trust his foe? The never artless
        pernicious dare, a catchphrase retweeted,
the taskforce debriefed at Camp Coalition.

Official permits are redacted. I picture their final
        gaze drifting into outback ley lines
from black mesas, stony winter lakes, desert frost.

Wind wraps each homicide in Koranic ash. Why not
        embargo Sharia law from the civilising canon?
Homesick for a country of neo-fascists & anti-Muslim
        provocations, in a country of empty schools,
water shortages and zero literacy, we do unto others
        because two hundred years of amnesia is
our excuse for genocide, because apostasy is our rule.

HOUBARA

Like the falconer, you prize her aphrodisiacs.
Shy, endangered bird, migrating from the steppes
to breed in the warm air of this Empty Quarter.

You imagine she fears a fleet of four-wheel drives,
campsites, the *majlis,* where a hooded falcon dreams.
How she dreads the tea boys' songs, a generator

droning all night long in the desert. By daybreak
the hunt begins. You search for evidence, while
a convoy chases her tracks, car phones screaming

over dry, rutted riverbeds, sprayed with Artemisia.
Like the falconer you've learned how to creep from
impotence to ambush, how the ground will surely

betray her, how a gyr untethered, sight restored
quickly gains height over her slow, deliberate
wingbeats. You watch him swoop to earth's face.

He points from the dunes, he circles her, melding
in a riot of awkward feathers. She cannot be twisted
back, her neck, a broken string he jabs in agony.

Dawn cauterises the sky. The falconer retrieves
her damaged carcass with a piece of chicken meat
to treat the hunter. You know his aftertaste of want.

Snow falls undisturbed in branches. The city refuses
to dream for sparrows, for park drunks, though it's past
midnight. Like a prayer, our moon waits to be spoken.
Once we chased Mallarmé's swan, dragging dissolute
wings into flight. Winter's amnesia preserved us –
unearthly swans, writhing in mud. Words broke their
baroque chords creaking in my nest of bones. You wrote
me tempting alibis, singing the frost, blotting out stars.
Night birds slumber. Stay – with arms unhinged, we'll
watch sparks flame as dancing roses, souvenirs of silence.
My body rivers over absent fields, where words rescue
or reduce me until I try to erase whiteness, her artefacts –
a snow-dusted angel of the lake, the symmetry of elms
undressing like brides in the night's incomplete sentence.

SWANS

Here in Orkney, they time-share as winter voyagers,
undisciplined pacifists, neither sentinel nor apsara.
A splash of colour on the bill is tarred as a birch leaf,
refusing to fall. The eye keeps faithful to her sky gods
knowing the powder of white water, the Nordic crags.
The throat's dying tone is a clarion, to which I woke
one arctic night, from my tent on the island. Against
the sky's green streamers they passed like gold leaf,
each captive pair, master and slave, returning to nest,
to feed on potato chats, the grain stubble. I knew then
no prayer or piety would convert these birds from patent,
territorial white. They are certain to hunger, to haunt
the estuaries in genetic script. There are no stichomythic
verses, no Viking battles or baptism in their dreams.

THE SIEGE

(In 1338, Agnes Randolph defended Dunbar Castle against the Earl of Salisbury)

Yellow is the complexion of spring – the celandine,
that brief invader, blanches to white. I would have
supped with the Earl who vanishes like a stag in fog.

Masons have camped in my donjon, miners hack
my gate; a husband is abroad, a brother is jailed.

Starvation winnows our meagre retinue of guards,
the fallow fields are in flame. Consider bridges built
over wild streams, a trebuchet fired at our bretasche,
how the roof subsides with the weight of flung stones.

Let maids dust off the ruins with their handkerchiefs
for the wind retreats, the swallows are in ecstatic flight.
Earth is moist. Ice melts in the ditches releasing buds.

Is it birth we want, or burial? Forget we stand in your
midst, hurling abuse. Unwilting, beyond resemblance.

It was school vacation, my daughter skiing with her father,
            my husband in board meetings,
mynah birds drumming on the window panes, autumn gifts,
            my dearest ex. in a condo in KL,
(true friendships don't crowd us, they are not a phrasebook.)

But it was just the grief I felt in his apartment, a stopover,
            sufficient to release claustrophobic
stanzas, one by one, a sorrow, unclenching its silence.
            Shopping at KL Central, the lap pool,
gymnasium, the trees peeling outside. I could call it respite –

forgiveness. I was at odds with bureaucracy, the clinics
            who treat psychiatrics like offenders,
gagging them with psychotropic drugs, they surfaced,
            gas-filled whales buoyed into my office.
While Indonesian boats sank their cargo, politicians waged.

I could write more – hours spent in earshot of innocent
            men tried by narrow halls, waiting for visas,
medical assessments or suicide. I could detail the security
            frauds, bribery, typhoid, children turned
by the hands of frustrated men like out-dated dictionaries.

Or I could mention the Rohingya Burmese father of four
            closing the door, in haste, unlocking
suitcases to scribble down their UNHCR-ID on the back
            of some food coupon, the sound of a hose
filling buckets of water for the day's quota; his exquisite wife.

Perhaps, I should confess how prohibited I felt, ferrying
            back to a 5-star hotel in evening's pollution,
encrusted lights of traffic. I had no appetite for dinners,
            swimming laps, late, without purpose.
Hibiscus swishes calmed my traitorous lungs – how I forgot
            everything I knew.

CHARLES DICKENS WEEPS FOR HIS LAST CHILDE

Beyond the coach, the open reaches of the Thames summons
ravens, gulls, otters, and the *Sussex* docked at Gravesend.

Mothers fiddle with their baskets and bonnets, children herd
cattle and goats, undaunted by din, the rank, soggy earth.

Autumn with her rich unleaving of oak, elm and maple
measures my bleakness. For days the wind has refused to speak.

My youngest, Plorn, waits in a boarding house with his dog,
his armoury of rifles, revolvers, saddles and family portraits

which will decorate the saloon. But when the fiddler plays a shanty,
when the sails are unfurled, the anchor raised out of mud

that other world begins with its nautical discipline. So remote
from landfall or the idleness of London, strange things can happen.

My advice is to write furiously in the evenings as Wilkins Micawber
– while shooting seagulls you may become your own fiction.

I'm fascinated by the arc of falling stars, eclipses, the way
words permit the undertow of shipwreck, gambling, child mortality.

I grieve for this farewell, to which my self is tethered, as letters
tied to pieces of coal are flung aboard a home-bound craft;

the voyage south to Melbourne both searing and cold. How still
the ocean is, a perfect fleet of ships, the distance quite imaginary.

HER DREAM

(Sarah Milligan was David Scott Mitchell's housekeeper until his death in 1907)

Tonight the same dream haunts me with veracity.
I wake to a dry storm. Trees creak, branches scrape
the eaves, a rat scuttles across the bearers. I hestitate
to light a candle, fearing the shadows books cast.
I've come to dread the borers, their cowled thorax.
Even as I speak silverfish and soft-bodied paper lice
quietly devour damp pages, undoing the bindings of
hundreds of fascicles I've yet to classify. Some days
I spend hours dusting manuscripts with broken chords.
I straighten the spines of incunabulum, trace rubrics,
run my hands over pared calfskin and vellum flyleaf.
The books choke the master's chamber, they emigrate
to the drawing room, stow a passage to the vestibule
so the entire north wing is jammed, floor to ceiling
with a curtain wall, a tumble-down turret of archives.
The master is anaemic, bedridden, but he sees visitors:
the broker Lennox Anderson, and staunch Mr Wymark
who carries promissory notes from convict records,
a botanist's journal of strange words I cannot read yet
try to love—for it is a grand affair, the master's library.
In the dream, I become an illiterate moth or a wingless
louse, pulverizing monographs to velvet dust, chewing
the starch that fixes leaf by leaf to the bondage of light.

DAY OF A SEAL, 1820

A tall ship patrols the coast,
                              the pelagic fish skirr.
I sniff the kelp and bloodworms,
                              mould into an eroded kerb
with a twist of neck, whisking as if
                              hiding my fur is natural
                              instinct for milk or man.

Tuesday afternoon, Bass Strait's shadows
                              ring the slaughter sands.
A man in sandals reeks as he wheels his rage
                              with a pivot, swings his heft.
A half-caste. I watch him clench the haft,
                              before the first blow shocks.
                              He braces and repeats.

Black women from the camps pile our skins
                              on spits for tobacco, for oil.
Some grab at birds with their gloves – Now
                              I am weightless as feathers
my arteries shut tight, as if underwater,
                              the acidosis bearable though
                              I cannot strike back.

TWOFOLD BAY, 1930

Then the curved tooth snaps with the tug of rope
in Old Tom's jaw as the Davidson's whaling boat
with its Yuin crew is hauled, freight harpooned.
The sharkskin skies have the mind of calamity.
A calf, not yet weaned, has been stalked, orphaned,
chased from the mouth of the Kiah at Twofold Bay.
Iridescent, the haven stretches from Eden to
South Head, an oily smell of herring is washed
adrift, coddled and simmering in endless quarrel.
The baleen's mandible is a fringed sieve, leathery
lips are neatly dissected, syllables of tongue
portioned, the fatty flesh verboten as Native deed.
Understanding is costly. Rib bones sold for collar,
corset, whip. Killer or feeder, tribal elder and kin,
rare milk of dreams, – the pectoral slaps reply
to Koori call, tail fins lathered. Wind stopples cold
on the whaler's spume-rinsed face – motorised boats
herald progress, shipping lines and wood chip mills.
Sixty fathoms of double coir are dragged out in play.
I can hear rope grind off enamel to a shiny groove,
feel his gums sting, the penetration, a split foreskin.
I see his country, fin keel and genitalia, the sharks
descend. There are photographs of his jaw, divergent,
the crags of his teeth are scales of instinct, force –
museums are white man's allegory but dreams of killer
and Koori whalers rewrite the past in undercurrents.
Steamships canon-fire harpoons ending the backwash.
Norwegian guns cull the pods of hunted Orca spirits,
bathypelagic ancestors. I can taste the words whiten
into thin milk of settler culture, bloodlines turnstiled.
Who would say the rookie cried 'What have I done?'
Who speaks of repose as a dry, ancient socket beached
on rock wharves, or as a carcass moored in the bight?

23

THYLACINE

When the palaentologist stepped over a creek bed,
to find in a hollow log my skull and rib mistaken
for wolf, fox or vampire he began to weep with guilt.
His sheep-grazing ancestors kept safe their ewes with

a bounty for each bullet-frayed pelt deserved curing.
Canine / feline / marsupial / carnivore – I confuzzled.
A cub's hind foot snapped. She was sold to London Zoo
in plaster of Paris slab, a few shipped to Coney Island,

or the circus tents. All the deals and export licences
distempered me, a shy beast, affectionate by turns.
The palaentologist knows economics cheated me,
a continent spread her legs to quarry the Tarkine frost.

Hunters and colliers became the new species, armed
with instruments, with cameras. But he is the future.
He glimpsed my pickled fœtus and like a god he came
into me – my genes a sludge, a chimera to clone back.

THE VANISHING

They hung me upside down
by the tail, molecules starched –
Irish trackers, old-timers.
I was tribal, a trophy locked
        with rigor mortis.

They forced my abysmal jaw,
my cough worthy of attention.
I would make no apology for stray
dogs who seized their pregnant ewes,
        if I could speak.

Dingos took blame for the cull.
I've seen the Youtube videos
of Benjamin calibrating hunger
to a charcoaled thirl, eyes barred,
        his hectored shadow.

How in God's name they shot a pack
of us, huddled with hungry cubs.
Sold a batch to Europe as domestics.
Kept me – as mascot, emblem,
        field study, postage stamp,

        zoology enigma
(stuffed on a taxidermist's plinth.)
When the last in captivity died
without too much fuss –
they dumped him in a paddock.

Have I slept for a week already?
A finger puppet in snow, a Visitorian?
The post-identity theory and cli-fi symposium
may never make amends. Before Twitter
        or the allegory goes viral

I'll escape into ferneries, veils of Time
from the experts, bureaucrats, Lake
St Clair's crags, from grotto to Sphinx,
jerking all the levers – till they
      vanish from my world.

PIROGUE

A boy, I dreamed of being a captain
in the ocean's foreign policy, catching
the fast currency, binding my pirogue
with a rope to hold back the breakers.

Listen. Today a jazz singer drowned,
the infringing Atlantic shipped pirates
to winch poaching flags as Senegal's
men scrape in the rotting sweatshop.

If only stories were like driftnets hurled
farther than Rosetta time but comets are
spun, desiccating colonies. And oceans
a chagrin, the frayed trellis of sardinia.

Our fish are émigres; there's no mercy for
the spawning flurry, our blood flows West
dragged undertow from Saloum to Seine
where Europe serves sovereign ministries.

Banks, NGO charities flog our sick children.
We'd starve if not for bushfood: tortoise or
dolphin meat. Our villages flood, leave us
licking silt-stained boabs, rum-soaked palms.

But I am one of Senghor's thin-legged,
migrant sons, too proud to beg for breadfruit;
hungry for Spain. Listen, today we threw
a decomposing body overboard – and prayed.

BEAR

The iceberg calved, trapping the belugas for
what seemed endless as winter, its crystal light.
I had been walking against wind, the blue ridge
of massifs, hungry, I had drifted towards the town.

I sniffed the dead seal, dragged it twenty metres
from the shed. My neck throbbed, I slugged air.
A boy on patrol whispered, jumpy, he smelt me,
the intruder, gave a warning shot and reloaded.

The Inuit know the fabric of my flesh, my pelt.
Our rule is eat or be killed, every tracker perseveres.
We are kin, forced onshore, it became a necessary
disruption, the quotas outdone, the ice melting.

This time I'm stranded, airlifted back to the floes.
Am I confused? I gash the whales but they dive.
No, I did not ask to be photographed on this plinth,
starvation and exhaustion have not cheated me –

I'll never forget the seal, the odour of his wet fur,
his smell altering mine, blood leaking from his heft,
like a river, discolouring the sanitation of snow.
Wind blasted the storm petrels. I could barely stand.

A ten-tonner skins by on a single lane, he swerves,
threading darkness, snow ploughs having shaven
the salt-sprayed road. He knows the moon's coin,
deer crossings, pine martens, every floating sign.
Sirens intrude with brash scintillations, an ambulance
cogwheels then locks to a brake. When police arrive
he's leapt free, scissored, ambushed by unreadable ice.
Radios freeze, phones tri-tone between GPS signals,
power cuts, fallen trees. Each hand-written envelope
is bundled, tied to the hope of tomorrow's promise.
Dawn permeates the valley. Trekkers set out from cabins
crevassed by minor narratives. Snow packs the ground,
covers the heather, the gorse bristles through bandaged
heath to map the terrain as powerlines vanish then
reappear. A stream's brown indentations reflect nothing,
end nowhere as unraveled time thins the bare willows.
Tractors drown in snow, the ruins of Roman walls are
buried pages. Pious sheep, marooned on frozen tussocks
watch as he arrives before the ferryman lifts anchor.
Drowsy at the turn, commuter to the girl with a smoky
dram reading letters by the hearth. His dreams undulate,
softly as snowdrifts cover skid marks, the day's spoor.

Sting of bramble, flags of Himalayan weed
have consumed the old packhorse trail,

as I hike, reason with breath, counting
each foot, carriage echoes deep in the valley.

The heavens rupture, bright above
the buttressed woods, stippled leaves initial

the sun's secrets in rose gold. Hauled up
over time's sediments, ruddy crags, a castoff

mattress copies the leaning quarry, hairline
fractured, where the wild grass is stone-walled.

To arrive is a peculiar risk, light veering,
wind hissing in the sycamores collects scraps.

Dog walkers shrug, a girl on a scooter, a boy
bouncing a ball. Here a housewife airs the bleak

expanse of myth and moor, aggrieved not by
routine, which might be quartz to the mind.

Know this world's indifference, charnel house
of bones to ration the earth's sacred plot, rivers

of peat, horse-drawn, gravestones erased, lifted
by storm as colossal trees wrest one casualty

from the next. Paramour or prey, God's lioness
or legendary swan who by gravity, resurrects?

The ash tree in the churchyard bleeds red berries
spilled and bruised, badly in need of cautery.

It hurts to accost death in her ruins, *Birthday*
Letters, pebbles from Devon, the shot-through asters.

Words, the bark of giant trees even a crow fears.
Plough the anatomy of songs into silence.

A man is knocking hard, unannounced, hoping
to make an appointment. He greets me as I return
from the library skirting mud, the damp grass.
Mary, the housekeeper is down with flu, our chef
is pumping weights at the gym. You are on a train
to London, a priceless alibi. And I, a village girl
in stockings, could be your messenger. I call to say
the surveyor has arrived to make an appointment.
Why can't he be a surveyor, today – I have in mind
a poem about Kafka's *Castle* but my sympathy turns
from Amalia to the vacant, water-damaged lodge,
where the carpet has been stripped and is ready
to be trashed like spam. While the man talks about
rewiring, I'm in your chair, surrounded by piles
of signed, handwritten letters from hopeful fellows.
I fail to mention rain dripping like sap from the lintel
beyond the drawing room where the river Esk
decants, bending back on herself, a gift returned.
I should pack or throw away tickets, receipts, maps
and pamphlets I've collected, but that seems dull,
a reminder of petty anxieties. Last night an invoice
arrived from Vodafone in two different countries.
I should take a walk along the river but can't face
the ice wind, the day's camera obscura, dark pines
along the ridge, the river's braided veins, the cold mare.
When are you coming back? you asked, last week.
I'm leaving tomorrow. Not waiting for the taxi. Not yet.
Yesterday, as we were blown to the tower, its corseted
window and gouged wall, snow beat against our faces,
too bitter for grief. *If you fall out there in the cold*
you could die. There's no point resisting: we can't stay,
each one of us, though what we seek is rest, we are restless.
The trees swither, say stop, soon the light will be lost.
I could walk by the river, even now – it's not too late.

LOSS

Dog otter, forgetful squire, how
long must I wait in this jumble
with my blind, translucent mess?

For the frenzied scent of hounds
rifles our holt, Norse pagans came
after you left – when I broke a little.

Our pups huddled, whined like birds
flummoxed as by the scruff I seized
each one, nudged to a nascent dive.

Baptised in algae, petroleum blooms
they flushed in the lake's oily shallows
to pop like velvet corks. Or lotteries.

Their fingers knot in prayer, suckled,
they dream of snow slides, shooting
weeds, the bladderwrack of your deep.

What have you plucked from mud?
I watch the homeless crows, eagles quiz
your riddle, my proxy, never-to-return.

Scraps swivelled, crushed fish-bone,
I sniff a little shuck of homecoming.
The wind blows musk into my dreams.

YOUTH, BY JOSEPHINE JAYSHREE CONRADY

Even as it recedes, why do I miss London?
Houses that reek of lime and coal smoke,
a crowded chaos spilling into Gravesend's
noisy piers, stevedores, a jungle of wharves,
dock gates, Tilbury's mastheads.

Determination is the better part of youth.
The arrhythmic sea pulsed in my blood
beckoning not the faint-hearted
for the North and the Atlantic fringe
these rocky shores, a nation
of headlands, islets and protectorates.

An orphan, my freedom was purchased
with a small allowance. At fifteen, flouting
the limitations of my sex I left my great
aunt's custody, her cardamom grove
in Pondicherry, and fled for the bustling
port city of Marseille with a copy
of Victor Hugo's
Travailleurs de la Mer.

I dressed in kurta with kersey breeches,
brass buttons, my hair clipped to the ears.
The sea beckoned, lingering
as in a dream, one does not wish to wake
from since it returns us to the cargo
of the drowned, unalterable past.

A harbour prays to the hurtling wind,
merchants, chandlers tally their yield.
My tongue was a chain of stray words
drifting, without anchor. When the skipper

instructed me I was silent and seemingly
like a dull child without imagination.
(But in my heart I was never a protagonist.)

Every voyage is a double voice, blurring
body and codex, buoyed by stars, cloud
vacillations, erasures of trade winds, every
harbour, a sentence. Myself, a foreigner:
so the folios of my adventures were sewn.

I spoke the argot of the navy: rosin, whale-oil,
cordage, hemp, windlass, hooks.
                    I caught the accents
of shore boat smugglers, spice traders,
I smelt the paraffin smoke of burning coal,
the bursting aromas of strange fruit, peppers,
the almond breath of slaves as we paddled
from our clipper to the shores of Mauritius.

Believe me, I had acquired a man's
strength, his firmness as one tossed to the
elements: incoming and embarking,
existing at the point of vanishing, being
ossified, where time is forever docked.

Wind clawed the waves, cabins creaked,
randomly the skies took pity, stars left
their scrollwork in the night, planets
were our portal. Skuas steered course,
scrawling their helical trace in the sky,
the day trembled with the sea's signature.

And suddenly we knew despair,
hunger, the fatigue of each breath,
the world a socket –
a thread of sirens enervating:

you return the wrong way, and all this time
the voyage, a scripture in grief,
the future's knot slipping through fingers.

Once, with small footsteps, I was a girl
tripping on the hem of her saree, towards
the bendy lines of latitude and longitude,
a youth charting passage on a wool clipper
from London to Freemantle, then Port Jackson.

There's only ever been one passage:
this deck I've paced, facing south.
this bunk I've curled up in, this loss,
my sixteen years, tossing rags into wrack.

What the eyes cherish comforts the heart:
a vast, cheerful harbour, bathed in sunlight,
though many a ship wrecked off her Heads.

          A shilling a month.
          Rations. Cold soup.
          Salted porridge.

We were docked in quay without a cargo.
The crew had abandoned ship.
I became a night watchman, invisible as death.

I walked the dirty lanes that tumbled
from George Street's littoral taverns,
its Chinese and tobacco shops.

Larrikins brawled with Arabs en route
to Melbourne. Police pointed bayonets.
Blackfellas camped on the fringe. Most nights
we drank a smoky malt, though English
consumed us all. English was a blank verse
that colonised our minds;
the full moon left us unbalanced.

The sea sighs and tintinnabulates.
It could strip a caulked stern.
We are deafened, we are sung by the wind.

To the lighthouse, south beyond riggings,
masts, buoys, towards the crops of Garden Island
a scene so peaceful, myself incidental.

Words scrabble. I piece them as a montage,
inlay after inlay. I fall in love with the bareback rider
of a travelling circus, write her as the paramour
of a minor character. I tinker with odalisques, tobacco
fields in Cuba. I feel the grip of a river's fingers
on my soul and trade dishonour for knowledge.
Always dreading how each story makes of me a slave,
despising the civilized plot underwritten by trade.

Youth is intrepid of all mystery.
She plys a corridor to the Torres Straits,
traces Cook to the Isle of Possession,
watchful around the Cape, for a gale
could smash the bulwarks, maul cabins,
shift the ballast. All day the endless toil
of shovelling sand, pumping water,
a feat, like life itself. Or futile words –
Black. Arabian. Baltic. Ivory. Atlantic.

The sea is restless for her prize, the reefs patient.
           Mercy we cry, each one of us
dreams of our poor carcass, swept asunder,
while in the harbour the hungry shipwrights wait.

Then one evening, after the gallery, hung with invisible
abstracts, you take me apart to flesh the miniatures:
a fleck of craquelure, speckles of mascara from my
        shadow eyes, already panda-streaked.

I fail to notice how you slip the pieces in your coat pocket.
Distracted as I am by wolf hands, the hairs in your cleft
neck. You're not, but you might be, up yourself, I think,
        skating across the vestibule floor.

How the light divides the dream, menacing, promising
shyness or indifference, I cannot tell, though it amounts
to the same verdict. Is that what you mean about pleading
        guilty as the fig trees stir, balmy in winter?

Some evenings are this fragile. Rainbow lorikeets court
the soft crumbs, a magpie takes off with a crust, clouds
skim over the Finger Wharf, footsteps trip in the Domain
        where the pine scent lingers as lips:

ours for a flower moment, the botanist's pinnate rose
is a name calling to its mute echo. Bats skip and loop
the legible sky in their quiet frenzy like involuntary
        kites between metallic and neon spires.

So dusk emulsifies desire, or maybe it's the reverse
– we are tenants of this periphrastic end. Office cubicles
half-lit, ladder the sky, turning their discretionary gaze
        to what's sketched by the carbon ink.

BEAUTY TIPS

for my mother

What words to fill the day? How to resist sentiment,
balancing dream and the recklessly blue sky?

Spring arrives with its allegro swell of trees, pollen,
a novel open on the kitchen bench, breakfast aromas.

Outside, the garden languors in laundry, agapanthus,
our swimming pool in need of chlorine turns emerald green

with insect wings, serrated jacaranda. What colour is truth?
I dip the soft sable in powder to dust away speckles,

cover shadows on my face, and yesterday's mascara.
Cleanse, tone, exfoliate. At all times, brush downwards.

I've disregarded my mother's beauty tips, her lessons
in permanence or grace. Her body slow, involuntary;

her eyes widened by Parkinson's, a fine tremor in the jaw
while the heart arranges, steady with belief and forgetting.

I take comfort in this. Mother, show me the other way back.
How the gravel is imprinted by the wind, by human steps.

Walk with me this evening, the sky crepuscular, rose-tinted,
the drifting scent of wild freesias like something strange,

half-known. You shuffle, sight weakened, wanting
to observe the fallen shingles, twigs, the scarcity of birds.

1

Under the sky's blue dome a man drags torsos
of gutted kangaroo to a soiled freezer, then he
hangs each sheath. Kelpies chained to half-buried
tyres lick the loyal dust. Bushflies helix at dusk.
Consider their rainbow lens, the compound eye
is unframed and swiped by hirsute, flexing feet.
Little colonisers, once farmed on Europe's dung.
Autumn winds come biting over tribal meridians,
raking syllables of country, of forty thousand years
barred by intrusions. On the rabbit-quarried dunes
blood money is history's hole, the lake is dredged.
Here in this gap, I flick a cigarette in the bone quiet.
If there's memory in my veins the ants carve it over
my body, edgy for a fix, or a verse the wind runnels.

2

Rock wallaby, fixed as a billboard in marbled
light, has fear branded in his genetic black box.
Stunned, where the river's veins intersect, his stare
dissects my theme (I could die of this feeling.)
What a curious theorist to guess the mammal in me
is more dead than alive, a trader, a slave to praise?
I sense him swither, swamp hero in the gloaming.
His ears retract. Involuntary, the mandible rises.
Before continents shifted, before orogenies split
the outer crust, marsupials thrived in Gondwanaland,
north and south. Earth revolved, our rafts burning
as we slept. Our giant forebears were no contest.
Kangaroos free-ranged, double-jointed koalas frisked
the eucalypts, Tasmanian dogs and devils prowled.

3

At night the stars are like termites or flying foxes.
A serial breaker of rules I entreat the ephemeral:
Borderline poet with GSOH seeks discreet patois.
Already the day bombards me with its brouhaha,
an empty vessel replete with signs. But nature
has a way of warning with an unplugged lyrebird,
or that discarded thong mouldering among leaves.
A sound of clap sticks and rifles seals the void's
tense silence. There are caves without hermits,
blackfella spirits hunted by firearms. Drugs fail,
my head's numb. A kayaker chalks the creek
yet, oddly, nothing disturbs the fictional granite.
The elegiac red gums restore calm and unwitting
sense to marginalia, trashing the mind's megabytes.

4

The river meanders from killing fields to half-light.
Never ceasing, nomadic running the scree. A lyric
festering, we ply her spirit with a destitute tongue.
Been fond of escape, been trading words for flight,
a bright skin of language, a second nature. Bring on
the sobriquets, take a few pills in the amber dawn.
I'm guessing the forecast is erratic, that dreaming
is my abode, but we have mansions for lovely forms.
We have harbour side galleries and Bindi Irwin.
Money jangles, and while it's hard to get this straight,
I'd swear by the riotous retort of raven or wattlebird.
Hear the mulloway leap with a hoary splash to shoot
the silence and you understand the fanatic – oh fish,
our common antecedent, remind us of difference.

5

There's a cave honeycombed by rain, a giant skull
blooming with tautologies, fallacies of superior race.
I'm twice in trespass. There's no changing, I can't
change, no, and there's nobody singing. I'm not
unkind or ignorant, but I'm here in this mould:
history's a genocide. The official site is vandalised
by love hearts, initials, millennium dates. And if
we miss the axe-grinding stones or petroglyphs,
do things simply vanish with our official deletions?
Even the trees were accomplices, persuaded to lie.
Wildflowers spill crimson wounds. What hunger
nourishes the starved rocks? Dusk is a blindfold.
The airwaves are carbon-free but I'm on my knees.
Time howls – the wind dries out every fresh crime.

6   .

At dusk, the ditching sun slips, burnishing the ridge,
its vellum of nervous silhouettes and veined leaves.
How many corners do we turn to ease this grief?
Our tongues swirl the tangled bark, we are cut by
barnacles, buffing a tarnished mirror to decipher light,
saving echoes from rhythmic whip of bird or wind.
We feel the ignominy of territory, we chase idioms
borrowed from culture, memory, the past's psychosis
and prison. Yes, there are words for this encounter
but insufficient love. Jet skis and fibreglass boats
speed by, their noise swift as our heeled soles press
hard the ground. The only path takes us from starlight
to stupor, the river in custody. Tribal tides wash
their black gravel over the oyster beds of this tribunal.

RECRUIT

Stranger, I have cried in my sleep for you –
my pupils smooth as nails hammered down.

Contingencies unspoken, like being homeless
or crashing after flight. I count the days in sobriety,

a missing number, the ocean's height configured
as if a swell is about to wipe me – a true fairy tale

of ordinary breath, a sunlit bay, a man secreting stars,
a mother whose arms are tied, a father's gun.

Afternoons sway to the pulse of a housekeeper's iron,
children dark and blonde are playing in the shadows,

the dull screens of appliances I've killed blank out
for an hour or two of forbearance, while

somewhere the earth is breaking. I am ready to run
from my words to yours, into the fault lines.

STORM IN THE HEART OF SUMMER

(after Neruda)

When he leaves her to take the ten bags of garbage down
       three and a half flights of stairs
to otto bins, the bottle shop, she leans against a windowsill.
Prayer flags billow in the wind, branches drift diagonally.

White-collar workers stroll to lunch, tobacco wafts, a mother
       pushes her pram up and over the curb
somewhere in the heart of summer. His shirt flags impatience
she measures in a glance, goodbye clouds shredding out to sea,

where the white caps resemble powder snow. He pours
       two kinds of wine. His bed is like the ocean's
grainy sheets, a cuttlebone's enamel with sepia script catches
the light, tendons ripple. She dreams in bouquets of coral

heliotropes, agapanthus deliriously cold, after rain. Maybe
       a girl is watching, writing her body
by the bright alcove, the afternoon filling with small birds,
exhausted by wind. The pavements confess to such crimes,

love and war alike in these chambers. Cranes haul their load
       with ropes and pulleys, plane trees
pitch their grenades, seeds the parrots missed, the day empty
as a page. Her hair's like sand blowing into cornflower eyes.

Waves wash the scent of trash, remove the sea's trinkets
       residues pooled in hollow caves.
So dark throats tangle, messy as a storm in mid-summer,
beating back time, the sting of words flying into eyes.

Before the light's particle rays pencil to floating
leaves, fingerlings, I've left him in a sea of sheets,
his dreaming, a cold waste. Abrasive snores drift
through snow blankets, underwater eyes unseen.

Deep to the surface a totemic legend rudders past
my coracle. I rest in wood rot, salt licking the skin
of my thigh. The scoop hem of a silk nightdress
with its black trimming ties flutters in the breeze.

Here a lamprey eel's stone mouth gapes in frigid
holes the ice composes like a riddle. A new moon
spares the sky's spectacle, intuitively reticent, or
maybe hardened by frost stars setting fire to the hills.

Birds begin to trill their silent score for late dreams.
The boat leaks, cloud water drawn in sapphire amulets
to wrap my limbs. Morning will sprinkle the conifers,
illumine map or dictionary, if not the treaty concealed

by my tarpaulin. I'd like to seed in a grave of mink,
Tuchone, buffalo bones, or in a deep nest where
sleeping fish wait to spawn. When the rapids come
and the wild crocus shoots, the inconnu will abandon.

For now, I am frozen, somewhere between aquatic
and terrestrial. I guess the river's arctic bend, imagine
nautical light, reading the smoke. Let wildfires reach,
groundwater springs rise; deadly, the snow melting.

FIVE SIJO FOR MY RAIDER

A sound of hooves over the dry stones of my sheets at night
My arms are withered, my bones rise to the quivering world
In the space between our thoughts are three aching syllables

My almost lover, no photograph of you, no goodbye note
Enemy, you have raided my country, your handwriting floats
Downstream through the forest, to the far walls of my kingdom

Your decrees are impulse, you enter without courtesy
And I become your dynasty, not knowing when to discern
death, by the penitence of leaves, by the haloes of traffic

In the far north, the river broke, bringing rumours of a tribe
I was alone that dawn, milking the soybeans, harvesting rice
With a bronze arrow you annexed my body to this design

Which of us abandoned the other? We cannot answer
How quiet the apartment: wind stirs, stars begin to shatter
Snow is a scherzo dancing over the words I've lost for snow

MINOR DOMESTIC

Jacarandas luxuriate
doused at dusk,
a xylography of fringed leaves
combs the barking
light.
Disabled elms sway,
the hedges ungainly, wield
to the drama of day.
A licence to renew, the house
aphasic, tangled: missing
marbles, a stapler,
wedge sandals strewn.
A half moon, flesh
flapping from knuckle,
like thumping, a detail:
ruby spurts in her room. How a child
dreams of sea-maidens
in tidal streams
while grown-ups carve
out the silence.

Magpies duet from a quivering syrinx, night echoes,
through windowpanes, the trees are inky whorls.
Solvents sully the stream with an astringent scent.

A porchlight shines its hard, fluorescent glare across pale
pebbly gravel, where, by day, feet tread and tyres crunch.

We are cautious of a mothering magpie's swoop.
Knowing her beak draws blood, we shun her gaze.
Telegraph poles and tall gums set precise co-ordinates.

I walk to the Falls, past lurid blossoms, wisteria clumps,
weatherboard maps of ivy. Birds go missing in this maze.

They forage among fields and roadsides waiting to ride
a thermal as morning thaws. I've heard their brief aubades
christen the dawn, their plangent, indecipherable calls.
In hunger or protest they weave the day's invocations.

The metaphysicians drive me outside to electric wrought
iron gates, the river's patois, her squirrel-scurrying syllables.
The sky is porous, bare stems flensing into thread bark.
Leaves spiral loosely from brassy sycamores, yellowing beech.

Do the dryads share my trivial anxieties: frosty lichen,
the disquiet of cloudy puddles, berries skating under boots?
A squall beats the trees in symphonic timpani, the spruces
drift in ribbons. Dark clouds brood and browse the valley.

Wind conducts me to the road where farm meadows duvet
in fallow, unploughed fields or the crudeness of rapeseed.
I might question my life in quatrains, the past ferries me back
to home in another hemisphere, to asphyxiating bushfires.

Past the stables, an inn, row-on-row of semi-detached abodes
with rear-entry drives, their gravel gardens, picket-fenced.
A few birthday balloons wield the wind, though the playgrounds
are vacant, a small knotted assembly shivers at the bus-stand.

I send a letter to my mother. At the library I read emails:
of course, there are pronouncements and petitions. Nevertheless,
not what I'd hoped for, but now life's commerce seems remote.
The wind is spiteful as I feed my foreign card into the ATM slot.

Too quickly the weathervanes turn. Schedules are in abeyance
street-side as everyone surrenders to the wreckage of wind.
I glance at shop fronts, pausing at the hair salon, café and bakery
but don't bother to enter. A storm could turn my hair to bracken.

Besides, coffee and a plate of scones can't halt the beating wind
on my walk back should I miss the bus. I could hitch a ride as
leaves are vestigial hands begging the sky for pity, that small word.
Antediluvian trees fur the horizon, the vertebrae of discrete hills.

Darkness falls abruptly. At first my eyes panic trying to test thes
calibrations. Pupils wide, the heart quietens a while before it stir
twilight spreads her crimson anecdote. I watch crows fraught
by evening's sacrament moan savagely. They carve the last ligh

DEATH IN BLOOMSBURY

All day I struggled with the ambiguous weather
as the sun blistered through uncut layers of cloud,
as wind shook the overhanging boughs of plane trees
which had forgotten how to caramelise their leaves.

By dusk I walked along the canal passing barges,
stray cats, cyclists, giant cranes, creels, geraniums,
granaries, lovers kept in sanctuary between locks,
girls in absurd heels holding hands, daisy saplings.

I had been thinking of Jacob Wainwright carrying
half a white man from Africa to Southampton Row
when, by coincidence, a friend appeared from nursing
her demented Mama. We bundled in the windy street

like dirty laundry, thirsting the future. It hailed swift
as a bullet embedded in the brains of a Syrian foetus,
precise as the quirk of meeting a stranger I once knew,
fatal as a woman being mugged while I drifted home.

I slept in a swoon, tipsy, tranquil, vomiting my words.
The night I was offered the world was the night I died.

A day that belongs to wind, dogs, farmers, colts,
to cranes migrating south in these autumn squalls.
This morning, a lull – for three hours the day was still.

Not completely static for a fieldfare weaved in the holly.
I saw the sprig quiver but failed to notice the mare graze.
The town bustled with its routine, stubbornly chores.

Smell the streets and you are reminded of sludge, coal
rising from underfoot, a rough odour that speaks of toil,
rain, of what feeds us in winter and keeps the town sane.

Hardly do we see the sun. Already it demurs, dark clouds
edge the horizon, the wind throws tantrums, indiscretions.
We are towed by its interior waves, obsessive as dreams.

Try as we may, we can't converse with wind. We can't
ask it to practise restraint. That would be too far-fetched
even for nature. Let the wind soliloquise into silence.

Let it be the tension between us. Today, it translates a
boy's ballooned trousers, a spaniel chasing a flock of gulls,
frayed plastic snagged by trees, an avalanche of leaves.

Just to be outdoors! To watch wind-tossed swallows rip
from private glens to common meadows, shaving the skies.
To hear fences grind, lamp posts screech, the oaks creak.

To be broken or to sing – which is our destiny? A bottle
jangles downhill, leaves scrape, watched by the psychic owl
as the wind's curved reflexion pours into abstract fields.

POSTCARD FROM CHILDHOOD

for Tegan

"When are you coming home, mummy?" she asks.
And I wonder where that is, walking by hoary light
to a bend in the road where the network transmits.

The drawing room is damp, radiators need bleeding
but breakfast is being served: porridge, hot tea, toast.
Routines shield us from a chaos we can't predict.

She's enveloped in evening's torpor. Cicadas drown
out television, bedtime stories pillowed with soft toys.
Distance, untimely seed of knowing, planted too early.

Nothing shelters us from memory, its tender waves,
nocturnal voices like postcards from childhood:
a thrum of ashoka trees, a Baptist preacher, dad's fault,

lagging after my mother's pram, toes numb, kicking
burnt autumn leaves around a statue of Thomas Coram,
graffiti beyond wrought iron fence, dirty slurries of snow.

The door knocks. You open to a gust of North Sea chill.
Partial facts, the years are swift as roe deers that stop still
then disappear – or bellbird notes sinking in the glade.

Footsteps echoed over towpaths, colonnades, squares.
Slung as cobweb strings, we are arrowed by light.
Birds shred the fraying sky in silent passage as we stir.

All morning, I watched how wind wrenches the trees.
Finally it shifted me from my seat, I should bend and bow
like the branches, with their heaps of peelings.
Nothing escapes change, being swept this and that way.
The crag is eroding, deeply scrawled in mud.
Engineers cannot save the red sandstone crumbled in time.
The architects' designs are archived on a damp shelf.
Even moss choses a path of gravity, greening the oaks.
The patient owl that wastes no effort will miss a prey
because the light tricks him and he hesitates. Too late.
Spruces point into shafts of light until clouds collide.
Buzzards wheel in warm thermals, but wheeze in hunger.
Deers graze when the valley folds into dusk, then fright.
I envy nature's economy, the mallard's flotation corrects
in the stream (though I've seen ducks drunk on toxins),
How do hawks enclose and stab with such symmetry?
Yet, routine alters for all living beings; our tendencies
are flaws, we grip like the cobweb, the leaf, the grass
before wind-stripping days, or horizontal rain sluices
the ploughed fields.
                              Some afternoons burn. I had felt
cruelty in the house, also tenderness. I swear you can hear
it in a man's voice when he speaks of the river's ostinato,
a fabled obeisance like ferns shivering in moonlight.
Into silvery mud I tramped, with wind-struck lips and wind
cold on my teeth. I saw the foam snagged by driftwood
disappearing into bubbles. It looked like blocks of ice.
Sheep spied me. Had snow covered the crest of the hills?
A farmer walked to her horses, quite alone in the fields.
She brushed them in darkness, threw oats over the fence.
The wind tugged at her mackintosh. I walked until my feet
drowned in slurry and every bare stem pointed the way.

ROSES FOR CRIANLARICH

These roses are not crushed or repentant.
Blood-scarlet, the petals sculpt time. Moments
slip by, a clock ticks, the refrigerator drones
and the iced-rain loosens in slow drips to earth.

Do they ask me to punctuate or unburden;
neither, or both in what measure? I am uncertain.
There is a road from Tarbet to Crianlarich, a low
pass to chase and patience are what one needs.

Keep your eyes wide for dark clouds stretch out
asleep in the heavens, as if they, too, hibernate.
Shut, like oyster bivalves fed to insomniacs,
how we dreamt of morning's pearl. Watch close,

if the road bends or narrows, if your luggage is heavy.
Nothing counts but the tramontane wind blowing
from the north. Nothing, but driftwood, are we;
so downy, the little ducks might teach us obedience.

Poor, spidery sepals affix the rose petals like arms
crossed for the clutching buds. There is a language
for each knuckle of mountain this sheer light held.
A language tramped this way and was made captive.

It was a summer of stinking heat, hellfire days,
nothing predictable but the violence of time
whistling throu a sou 'westerly, the dragon lizard
scampering to underbrush from crops of dry lawn.
Boxes in every half-filled room, masking tape rolls,
anarchic cockroaches slewing between floorboards.
I learned how to correct grey hair roots, presbyopia,
leaking showers. The marriage laws defied me.
Then one tradie after another, phone calls, texts.
In my alacrity, I'd confuse their names, driving from
Canada Bay to Lidcome, Ikea to Parramatta Road
for blackbutt, bamboo, terracotta. Scott from Prospect
gave a quote I accepted for all the drop sheets, all
the brawn and Epoxy sealant it took to keep me single.

CAR LOVER

It can be healing to walk the vacant streets
of these suburbs, over tree-buckled pavements,
the ground cicatrised, I'm a proverb of missing
woman with tablet, with handbag evidence.

It can be therapy to loiter in the park, streetlamps
glow with yellow discernments though V8 utes
may be scarce, the road rule is swift and strobic.
The sky is gagged but I'm a sentence in heels.

Trees camber, pencilled in mist, row by row.
Cars gear in / out of driveways front or rear-ended
with gear-stick discovery. A frogmouth cautions me,
the rose-lit church grounds pray for my flesh.

Consider me slumped cold against a brick wall.
What device pedals thought's accessories?
Cars sing hosannas for the freeway, pulsing
nocturnal. I improvise, I turn like leaves rasping.

Dumped by sleep's apparatus, there is a girl who
beckons from below the liquidambar. I've heard
her chafing. Bring an ice pick. Send a coupé to
abduct me, my bones whistle of that other Spring.

After dinner he was bashed by an Islander
at Circular Quay, because I looked fresh
and he was antique white, his hair receding.
I remember him fumbling for his glasses
among heels on the ice-cream-stained pavement.
The policeman at The Rocks took affidavits,
such small interference in the prescribed light.
(I counted imperfections in the mock terrazzo.)
We went back to the hotel, slept like octopedes
till I left, unnerved, and he flew out. The smug
Miss at reception glared at me like I was a huss
so I wiped my blush, the silver hoop earrings.
That was my twisted shit; I guess we strayed
too close to the jetty sinking in the lapsed night.

CASTRATO

When the kitten with a dislocated limb is euthanized,
you've stopped reading my blog, my sister refuses the call,
a bargirl on the south side of Sydney is being shagged,

when every contract is optional, the Ping-Pong game is over,
the flat day reeks of a stinking premonition on the pretext of
afternoon teacake, vanilla-iced, served with the luminous smiles

of a stay-at-home mum to reprise me of the stakes I've gambled,
make-up too bright, or remind me Falciparum malaria hooks up
to maggots glossing the trash heaps on Manus Island, page 6 –

when the slush pile of supplier statements, invoices, failure-to-pays
I've ignored becomes a pylon, having clocked up as many as twelve
angry men who'd expect equality and dignity are unconditional?

When I've almost crossed the desert hallucinating Lasseter's cave,
with a parasitic strangle when poetry raids every layer of self-respect
so I can no longer read newsprint, let alone the opening sentence

of my tenth surplus draft, syllable by syllable – I'll start over like
a teenage boy with secret admirers in the back seat of his mother's
4WD, learning to curse before my voice breaks for the first time.

Morning's fluke obscurities deepen the room.
The trees are clenched outside. After REM
I endure hours minus sedatives or morphine.
(Where's my Doctor's Bag when I most need it?)
What a waste of credentials. I draw my lame
self out of my pyjamas, think Nijinsky slithers.

On the bar fridge, pre-alarm, swipe the iPhone
Hey world, what's out there 2day? Hope just
can't be quelled and punishes me with a habit:
check windows live mail, FB, site stats, country
by country, whisper sync. Savannah has messaged,
there's a missed call from LA Mike on Skype.

Remind Sanjay he really ought to fix his webcam.
He lives in Nehru Place, goddam it, right next to
a semiconductor giant. Would like to see his face
when we talk and I expose my fragility to the blue
lit-LED monitor with full H-res. It's strange how
I'm astonished that sweet, fetching avatar is me.

Cup my face in my hands. Feel the river of grief
wash through. Don't admit freely to the Tinysex
that blissed me last night – such pretty eyewear.
Swear I'd never chat or moderate but I don't crave
real life much these days. For my very own eccentric
Russian accent, copy Dostoevsky's *Idiot* to Kindle.

SEA OCTAVES

Tiny holes in the sand
      made of the creeping
punched in darkness –
      excavations, crabs shuttle,
fugitive worms, ectomorphs
      who escape the pump.
Does the sea flush away
      the darkness of holes?

Undulating wholeness,
      fine-drawn, a tireless flow
of liquid, spray, ice.
      All this shell is memory –
purling the cerulean.
      Inarticulate crustaceans
at whose insistence do
      you sing beyond words?

Water glissando, the inchoate
      waves fugue, unfetter
pulverise a salty grammar
      sargassum, slapped and stray.
A trio of barnacle, rose, kelp –
      the littoral is cold adagio.
Once, the blue ice creaked
      dimly sounding its name.

No tripping in the aleatory light, no thesaurus
for radioactive dusk with incurable ciphers.

I was in a ruck, hinged when the world broke.
Not least the prick of the tattoo needle
on the page, desultory as a gammy rice field.
                No empty styrofoam riposte.
No token, no portal, no slot.
My *zuihitsu*... ask the one-way paramedics.
                   Float like a mask in tsunami.
Self-reflect as acidic nuclear shadows
adrift with refrigerators, bicycles, terns
half-buried in sand, sloped Coca-Cola blazon.

All that remains is the running brush, a train
and a whisper in the machine, half-wilting.
No figures of speech – nothing to speak of.

FOUNTAIN 77

(Glebe Point Road)

Plastic-sheathed roses embroider the dark.
Set to volplane
we take photo-triptychs, each of the other.
Moments of daring oscillate in the strangers
we become.
And arms betray us,
they link our assembly of states, ventriloquised,
cravassed by cloud, echoes, reason's
sastruga faults, whole continents of inaccuracy
rumoured, unrumoured.

Making for the 336, syllables cleft as we inhale
olfactory flakes, a wrapping scrapes the asphalt
in our roan-coloured quarter.
Parting, of course, is not
sinking like some Titanic hybrid, cobalt-feathered
favouring métissage,
but a cold coming –
so riddled are we?

MUMBAI BY NIGHT

for Sharlene

After I sent you the text and there was silence
it occurred to me it felt like a wave about to break.
Last time I heard your voice startle – hesitant as
though you'd guessed I could drown in that suite
they'd upgraded me into because cocaine addicts
were flipping, trashing the next room. I was so high,
you knew our drinks were spiked with ice, that I'd
switch amnesia for insomnia, *No wake-up*, please,
that soon enough the Mumbai dawn would flood
the glazed facades of the thirty-something floor, a
miasma of smog over the Dharavi slums, the marsh
redevelopment, the Indiabulls and Oberoi towers.
That I'd catch my flight all the way back to oblivion
until the next stop-over. Assuming your Bollywood
diva permits, we'll take a ride to *Tryst* in Lower Parel,
you'll smoke in the heat of a taxi, windows down,
talk boys and dance to the electro house screen as
overweight brokers and expatriates admire. Or else
we'll drink tequila, eat takeaway with your old man,
avoiding awkward questions while filling in the gaps
for what little we know of each other. Let's face it,
however easygoing you seem I'm like any foreigner
you're obliged to entertain, one who has finally
acquired the sense to keep her opinions unpacked.
We may never wake in the same room again, unsure
if I should go to Goa with you or chance a rebel poet
in Chhattisgarh. I guess the disparity between my
intensity, jet-lag and your street glamour won't ever
change. Time is a fixed currency without counterfeit,
so brief it leaves me cheating myself with words.

Afterwards, Jiah Khan slung her red silk dupatta
from a ceiling joist in her Juhu beach apartment,
my viral-stricken buck rattled to sleep curled by
my bed, and I woke to the cold body of silence –
to rumouring eucalypts while outside field mice
scampered, their brood coffled by a tomcat's spur.
Wine in the bay, the casual emptiness of dusk
spilled like words flooding my dry, jittery veins.
I lay restless: half-alive, a tinder to your hexing
syntax, indefensible, a trauma of prayerful hands.
Morning's atonement was a church in Assagao,
radio salsa, a driver who pitied my émigré faith.
Every step was littered. There was a flower cart
left, a crucifix half-buried in the scarified earth.
I peeled in that oasis of clean light, Manueline
arches encircled the red patchwork of reliquaries.
Conceiving rosary beads I read tablets of duplicate
José de Souzas and Catharine Théresas of Lisboa,
and in folly traced a snake to the locked presbytery,
its archives stained with sweaty imprints, *vinho*
– later, Conceição de Jacinto, head of forgeries
avowed a nine per cent rise in adulterated passports.
Now darkness is awash, I burn sandalwood without a
care for genealogy scams, the predictable everlasting.
Shredding basil, I stir. I drink wine alone, tallying
the fixed unanswerable syllables, this arid cursive,
sure oblivion, a dying of desire; of fading, not dying...

THE END OF THE DREAM

(after Wallace Stevens' 'Of Mere Being')

You squint, turning the pages of a quarterly,
half-dozing, in and out of centre, well beyond
the Socratic itch or the circadian persuasions.
Look over your shoulder, a gesture held by dusk
to observe no gold-fangled bird but a palm tree
raking the fragile skies, singular and eternal –
with a movement so discreet it begins to thread
the light, you are almost stunned not by melancholy
but the hallucinatory moment years have spent.

Frogs moan, eucalypts pixelate in dark stirrings
that come much later; and should a formal music
drop it would be a flat line in reason's anaesthetic bed.
You remember the stained glass, cathedral pines,
fragrant star jasmine infuse the pages of a culture war,
there are hunger games and Israel blitzing Palestine.
Unfamiliar rooms inhabited, a Fushan sandalwood
rinses the air, the scalene triangle of three solicitors,
all sides unequal, a tenant needing a dog-proof fence.
Now your ex-boy is a landlord, your mother's body
dry and papery like snakeskin shed past midnight
when a bird with tawny feather hair extensions quips.
At the end of the dream, a garden bench presumes
the child has outgrown you, a jacaranda shakes her thick,
purple amnesia, predicting what makes us happy
                                        or unhappy.

p. 13 'The Edge of Empire':
gromatici were land surveyors in Roman times, named after groma, an instrument which they used for surveying.

p. 15 'Houbara':
majlis is a meeting, a place of sitting (in Arabic)

p. 19 'Her Dream':
Sarah Milligan was David Scott Mitchell's housekeeper until his death in 1907. Mitchell was a book collector, the founder and benefactor of the State (Mitchell) Library in Sydney.

p. 21 'Twofold Bay, 1930':
Old Tom was one of the best know Killer Whales, whose cooperation with Indigenous and settler whalers in south eastern Australia between 1840 and 1930 came to a dramatic end.

p. 61 'Castrato':
Harold Bell Lasseter, was an explorer who purported to have discovered a rich gold belt in Central Australia sometime between 1897 & 1911. The 1930 expedition to relocate the gold 'reef' failed, and Lasseter died alone in the desert, his party and camels having left him.

p. 64 'After Fukushima':
This poem takes inspiration from 'A Girl Ago' by Lucie Brock-Broido.

MICHELLE CAHILL was born in Kenya, lived in the UK and resides in Sydney. Her poems have been widely anthologised. She has received grants from the Literature Board of the Australia Council; she was a Fellow at Hawthornden Castle and at Kingston University, London. Her prizes include the Val Vallis Award and the Hilary Mantel International Short Story Prize. She was highly commended in the Blake Poetry Prize and was shortlisted in the Victorian Premier's Literary Awards and the Newcastle Poetry Prize.

My thanks to the editors of the following journals where some of these poems have appeared:

'Second Winter' in *Antipodes*; 'The End of the Dream' in *Arc Poetry Journal*; 'The Dying Art' in *Australian Book Review*; 'Night Birds', 'Bear' & 'Thylacine' in *Australian Literary Review*; 'Storm in the Heart of Summer' in *Australian Poetry*; 'Interlude', 'Day of A Seal, 1830', 'The Vanishing' & 'Pirogue' in *Cordite*; 'At Blackheath' in *Crannóg Magazine*; 'Real Life' & 'The Castle' in *Island*; 'Beauty Tips' & 'Charles Dickens Weeps for His last Childe' in *Jacket2*; 'Swans', 'Houbara', 'Her Dream' & 'Loss' in *Meanjin*; 'Castrato' in *Overland*; 'Somewhere a River' in *Pennsylvania Literary Journal*; 'Mumbai by Night' in *Peril*; 'Harbour', 'Wind' & 'Death in Bloomsbury' in *Shearsman*; 'Roses for Crianlarich' in *Poetry Scotland* online; 'The Siege' & 'Taboo' in *Southerly*; 'Heptonstall' in *Rabbit*; 'Twofold Bay' in *The London Magazine*; 'Fountain 77' in *The Disappearing, a Red Room Project* and *The The Poetry*; 'After Fukushima' in the *Red Room*; 'Renovations' in *The Age*; 'Insiders / Afghanistan' and 'Night Roads' in *The Wolf*; 'Surveyors at the Edge of Empire' in *Wasafiri*.

Some of these poems appeared in the following anthologies:

'Recruit' in *Australian Love Poems 2013* (ed. Mark Tredinnick, Inkermann and Blunt); 'Swans' and 'Night Birds' in *30 Australian Poets* (ed. Felicity Plunkett, UQP); 'How the Dusk Portions Time' in *The Best Australian Poems 2011*, (ed. John Tranter); 'Renovations' in *The Best Australian Poems 2013*, (ed. Lisa Gorton); 'The Herring Lass' in *The Best Australian Poems 2014* (ed. Geoff Page); 'Bear' in *The Best Australian Poems 2015* (ed. Geoff Page); 'Car Lover' in *The Best Australian Poems 2016*, (ed. Sarah Holland-Batt); 'Swans' in *The Turnrow Anthology of Contemporary Australian Poets* (ed. John Kinsella, 2014); 'Hemisphere' in *Dazzled*, University of Canberra Vice-Chancellor's International Poetry Prize Anthology (2014); 'Car Lover' in *Anthology of Contemporary Australian Feminist Poetry*

(ed. Bonny Cassidy & Jessica L Wilkinson, Hunter, 2016.)

'How the Dusk Portions Time' was commended in the *Aesthetica* Poetry Prize 2011; '*Youth* by Josephine Jayshree Conrady' and 'The Grieving Sonnets' were both shortlisted in the 2012 Newcastle Poetry Prize, and both appeared in *Coastline*, the prize anthology (eds. Kim Cheng Boey and Jennifer Harrison).

I am grateful to Hawthornden Castle for a Fellowship in 2011, for a poetry Fellowship at Kingston University, London awarded by the Copyright Agency Limited and the University of Wollongong in 2013. My thanks to the Literature Board of the Australia Council for a Developing Writer's Grant awarded in 2013 and to the Australia Council for a publishing grant in 2015.

My thanks to A. M. Bakalar, James Byrne, Angela Jarman and Tony Ward.

This project has been assisted by the Australian Government through the Australia Council, its arts funding and advisory body.